"All the President's Men and Women"

The Secretary of the Treasury
through
Lloyd Bentsen

John Hamilton

Published by Abdo & Daughters, 4940 Viking Dr., Suite 622, Edina, MN 55435.

Library bound edition distributed by Rockbottom Books, Pentagon Tower, P.O. Box 36036, Minneapolis, Minnesota 55435.

Cover Photo by: AP/Wide World Photos.
Inside Photos by: The Bettmann Archive (8, 9, 11, 15, 19, 21, 25, 27, 28)
AP/Wide World Photos (5, 12, 14, 17)

Edited By: Sue L. Hamilton

Library of Congress Cataloging–in–Publication Data
Hamilton, John, 1959-
     The Secretary of the Treasury / written by John Hamilton
          p.   cm. — (All the President's men and women)
     Includes bibliographical references (p. 31) and index.
     ISBN 1-56239-254-9
     1. United States. Dept. of the Treasury. Office of the Secretary—Juvenile literature.
2. Cabinet officers—United States—Juvenile literature. [1. United States. Dept. of the Treasury.
Office of the Secretary. 2. Hamilton, Alexander, 1757-1804.]
I. Title. II. Series.
JK261.H327   1993
353.2—dc20   93-11214
                                                                        CIP
                                                                         AC

Printed on Recycled Paper

CONTENTS

The President's Cabinet: An Overview

When someone is elected President of the United States, he (or she) immediately takes on a huge amount of responsibility. Presidents must oversee all laws passed by Congress. They're the head of the armed forces. They must decide foreign policy–how should the U.S. help its friends and allies, and how should we punish our enemies? If the economy stumbles, the President must try to get it back on the right track. Presidents must make sure that laws are handed down fairly; energy is used wisely; parks and other government lands are put to proper use; citizens are educated, put to work, and kept healthy. And that is just a small part of what Presidents do!

Obviously, no one person, no matter how smart, can possibly know everything there is to know to do a President's job. A President paints in broad strokes, deciding the tone and direction of how the country should be run. To help with the details, the President has a "cabinet" a group of people to meet with regularly for advice on important decisions that must be made every day.

There's no law that says the President must have a cabinet. It's a system that has evolved by custom over the years. The United States Constitution says that the President "may require the opinion, in writing, of the principal officer in each of the executive departments, upon any subject relating to the duties of their respective offices." But the President doesn't have to ask their advice, and doesn't have to go along with what they say if the President thinks they are wrong.

The heads of these cabinet departments are called "secretaries" and are appointed by the President. The Senate checks the secretarys' backgrounds and votes on whether to accept them. Nominees are picked for their experience and special talents in the areas they are to oversee. Only rarely is a President's pick rejected. After the Senate accepts, or "confirms," cabinet secretaries, the President alone has the right to remove them if unhappy with the way they are performing their duties.

When a President resigns or is defeated in an election, the entire cabinet also resigns. New Presidents can rehire old cabinet members, but they usually want their own trusted advisers to help them run the country.

This book will focus on one of the oldest and most important cabinet departments, the **Department of the Treasury**.

President Clinton presides over his first Cabinet meeting in the Cabinet Room of the White House.

The Secretary of the Treasury

The Secretary of the Treasury is the President's main advisor when it comes to anything having to do with money. The Secretary recommends financial and tax policies that have broad effects on America's economy. The Secretary also keeps an eye on our national banking system, making regulations when necessary.

Over the years, there have been many plans to keep our economy running at full steam. Some Secretaries believe that citizens should be taxed more so that the government can spend more, which they think makes the economy stronger. Other Secretaries think people should be taxed less because over-taxing the citizens makes the economy slow down. Others believe in what is called "deficit spending," which means the government spends more than it takes in from taxes. While this speeds up the economy in the short run, it creates the problem later on of how to pay back the money the government owes (the "national debt").

To understand this better, think of what happens to some families around the holidays: There's not enough money to buy nice presents for everybody, so Mom or Dad buy gifts with a credit card (deficit spending.) This makes for a nice holiday season for the whole family. (The economy has been speeded up for the short term.) But soon the bill arrives, showing just how much the family has overspent (the national debt.) How should they pay off this debt? Usually, it can't be done in one big payment; it has to be spread out over several months. But then the bank charges interest on the amount we still owe. We end up paying more than we would have if we'd just paid cash back when we bought our presents. So it's best to pay off debts as quickly as we can. How? Cut back on everyday things for a while? Take another job?

On a much, much bigger scale, the Secretary of the Treasury has to deal with our entire country's economy. At the beginning of 1993, our national debt was over four trillion dollars! (That's $4,000,000,000,000.) That's one big bill, and it's the Secretary's job to figure out how best to pay it off. Obviously the President wants someone to head the Treasury Department who is very smart with money and the economy.

Figuring out economic policy is just one of the major jobs of the Secretary of the Treasury. The Treasury Department is actually a collection of several offices, each with its own different function. As head of the Treasury Department, the Secretary is responsible for four main areas: making economic policy; serving as a financial agent for the United States Government; enforcing the law; and making coins and currency.

The most important job for the Secretary of the Treasury, of course, is to make policies that will improve our nation's economy. The Secretary is responsible for figuring out and recommending to the President how the United States should collect and spend its money. This is called "fiscal policy." Many different decisions must be made to form a fiscal policy, which include raising or lowering income taxes, managing the public debt, and deciding on import and export taxes (called tariffs).

As a financial agent for the United States Government, the Secretary is on many government and private boards, commissions, and councils. Most of these groups are very powerful, with impressive-sounding names like the International Monetary Fund, the Economic Policy Group, and the International Bank for Reconstruction and Development. When these groups meet, the Secretary of the Treasury makes sure that the opinions and positions of the United States are stated, understood, and upheld.

The Secretary oversees two other big functions of the Treasury Department: law enforcement and the minting of coins and printing of paper money. These two areas will be covered in more detail later in this book.

History of the Treasury Department

The United States as we know it today began in 1789, when our Constitution went into effect. In that year, Congress passed laws that created the first three Executive Departments, of which the Treasury Department was one. (The other two were the Department of State and the Department of War, which later became the Department of Defense.)

When our first president, George Washington, started looking for America's first Secretary of the Treasury, he knew he needed someone with a great business sense, someone who could get our small economy running strong. Washington chose Alexander Hamilton, a New Yorker who had worked closely with Washington during the War for Independence and who had pushed for a strong national government. As the new Secretary of the Treasury, Hamilton immediately took steps to put America on a sound financial footing, including creating a national bank and paying off the national debt.

Alexander Hamilton.

Originally, the Treasury Department was responsible only for managing America's finances. But as time passed, the Department's duties expanded to include a number of important functions, which we'll explore in the next chapter.

Other Responsibilities of the Treasury Department

The Treasury Department is really a collection of departments, each with a different function. The Treasury Secretary decides, in broad strokes, the direction these departments should take. The heads of the different departments then figure out the details.

United States Mint

An important thing happened when the Constitution took effect: The United States would have only one kind of currency for the entire country. To make this currency, the United States Mint was started in 1792. Then and now its main purpose is to make the coins that we use for money. Ever since it started, all the coins in this country have been made by the Mint and the Mint alone.

There are two functioning mints, one in Philadelphia and one in Denver, plus the Old Mint in San Francisco. In addition to making coins, the Mint also makes all medals for the government.

Making silver dollars at the Denver mint.

These are given for acts of bravery in times of war or for special service to the country.

Another job of the United States Mint is to make sure the Treasury Department's gold and silver supplies are safe. Gold is kept in Fort Knox, Kentucky, and silver stored at West Point, New York. These bullion supplies are controlled by the Mint and protected by the United States Army. When the United States has to pay debts to other countries (many times they take only gold or silver for payment), the Mint arranges to transfer the bullion. These transfers are done in great secrecy.

The U.S. Mint has public exhibits and sales areas at the Philadelphia and Denver Mints, the Old Mint in San Francisco, and Union Station in Washington, D.C. Admission is free.

Bureau of Engraving and Printing

Just as the United States Mint makes our coins, the Bureau of Engraving and Printing makes our paper money. And that's not all: the Bureau designs, prints, and finishes a large variety of security products, including Federal Reserve notes, U.S. postage stamps, Treasury securities, identification cards, and certificates. It is also responsible for helping other Federal agencies in designing and producing other government documents.

The Bureau is the largest printer of security documents in the world. (Over 40 billion are printed each year.) Printing all that money involves a lot of secrecy to make it harder to counterfeit. The making of paper money was authorized in 1862 during the Civil War, and since that time only one company has supplied the paper for the currency. It's manufactured from a secret formula known only to a handful of trusted people. Printing of the money takes place in buildings in Washington, D.C., and in Fort Worth, Texas. People who work in these printing plants go through tight security checks. Visitors are welcome to come watch the money being made, where they can see millions of dollars in huge sheets of money rolling off the presses.

Printing dollar bills in Washington, D.C.

An agent of the Bureau of Alcohol, Tobacco, and Firearms stands guard at the Branch Davidian compound near Waco, TX. ATF agents were involved because cult members were using illegal firearms.

Internal Revenue Service

The Internal Revenue Service (IRS) is probably the most well-known of the Treasury Department's sections. It is responsible for collecting the taxes that the Federal Government decides U.S. citizens must pay each year. No one is allowed to fail to pay their fair share of taxes, and the IRS makes sure everybody obeys the law. The United States is a huge country with millions of taxpayers. To accomplish its task, the IRS has offices in every region of the country and employs thousands of workers.

When tax forms come to the IRS offices, they are checked by computers to make sure no mistakes are made. If an error is detected, action is immediately taken to correct it. Sometimes the IRS must file criminal charges against people who refuse to pay their fair share. On other occasions, though, a taxpayer may have made a mistake and paid too much. The IRS tries to make sure that this person gets the proper refund.

Bureau of Alcohol, Tobacco and Firearms

The Bureau of Alcohol, Tobacco and Firearms (ATF) was started in 1972. It enforces laws that have to do with guns and explosives, as well as alcohol and tobacco products. It also investigates cases of arson where buildings are burned down and the owners make a profit from their insurance. The enforcement of these laws used to be the responsibility of the IRS, but the amount of work demanded that a separate bureau be formed.

The ATF is headed by a director in Washington, DC. But like the IRS, the ATF has offices in every region of the country. In recent years firearms have become a serious problem in our society. We have laws that say what kinds of guns we may own and how they may be used. Criminals, however, are not interested in obeying these laws, and use their guns to rob or kill other people. The ATF's job is to track down people who sell and use guns illegally.

The ATF also tracks down people who make liquor with illegal "stills." People who make liquor outside the Federal regulations and sell it on the black market are called "bootleggers." Not only does the government lose tax money from these unauthorized stills, the bootleggers often make their liquor in an unsafe way, making it dangerous for consumers to drink. The ATF tries to track these people down and put them out of business.

The ATF is also responsible for stopping illegal gambling, arson-for-profit, and the selling of stolen cigarettes.

United States Customs Service

The U.S. Customs Service collects taxes from goods that are imported from foreign countries. This is to protect American companies from low-priced imports. If you enter the U.S. after a trip from another country, the Customs Service makes you declare what goods you've brought back with you.

In addition to collecting taxes on goods entering the United States, the Customs Service also has law–enforcement responsibilities. Here, a Customs agent unloads kilos of cocaine after cutting into the deck of a small boat, removing more than 1,000 pounds of smuggled cocaine.

A U.S. Customs agent stands behind $2.1 million dollars of U.S. currency that was seized after money launderers tried to smuggle the money into Canada by car.

People are allowed to bring in small amounts of items, but if you bring in too much you have to pay a fee.

The Customs Service isn't just a tax collector, though. It also has law enforcement responsibilities. It makes sure people don't bring in contaminated food, plants or infected animals that may harm citizens in the U.S. It also tries to stop illegal drugs from entering the country. Customs inspects foreign imports to make sure they are safe and comply with our labeling laws. They also help enforce laws against ships that pollute American waters with refuse or oil.

The Customs Service has its main office in Washington, D.C., but it is found all along the borders of America, in all seaports and airports, keeping watch for Uncle Sam and the Treasury Department.

United States Secret Service

The Secret Service was started in 1860 and given the important job of protecting the American people against counterfeiters. It seemed natural to place this Service in the Treasury Department. Most of today's Secret Service still deals with fight against counterfeiters, arresting people who forge coins or currency.

The Secret Service is better known for protecting Presidents from harm. The Service started this job after the killing of President McKinley in 1901. This protection has now been extended to the vice president, president-elect, vice president-elect, major presidential candidates, and former presidents and their families.

Next page: Despite meticulous planning and care by the Secret Service, tragedy can occur. In 1980 a lone gunman got through security and shot at President Reagan as he was leaving a Washington, D.C. hotel. President Reagan waves, top, then looks up, center, before being shoved into his limousine by secret service agents after being shot.

With the growth of terrorism around the world, the Secret Service has become very diligent about protecting the President and his family. In the White House, even on Christmas when the First Family opens their gifts, Secret Service agents are always on duty, just outside the door.

The Secret Services tries to think of everything when it comes to protecting the President. When he is out in public in a potentially dangerous situation, they make the President wear a light bulletproof vest. Cars and trucks full of Secret Service agents, armed with machine guns, follow every presidential motorcade. When the President shakes hands with crowds of people, the Secret Service has many agents in the crowd, on the lookout for anybody who might try to harm him or her.

Biographies

Alexander Hamilton

Look on the front of a $10 bill and you'll see a portrait of our first Treasury Secretary, Alexander Hamilton. George Washington chose Hamilton to be America's first Treasury Secretary because, not only was he a trusted advisor, Hamilton also had a keen sense of finances and strong ideas on how to get the young country's economy running strong. He was a master of power politics, and used his influence to go beyond finances to include foreign policy and social planning. Hamilton had the foresight to realize that America would become a strong world power by shifting from a farming society to an industrial society. His economic plans tried to make that change easier.

Hamilton was a small, slender man, with light hair and deep-set eyes. Some found him to be vain, even arrogant, but friends knew him as warm and loyal. He was very ambitious and hard working, and a skilled writer.

Alexander Hamilton, America's first Treasury Secretary.

Hamilton had humble beginnings. He was born in 1755 on the island of Nevis in the British West Indies. His father, after moving his family to the island of St. Croix, abandoned them. Hamilton's mother was very poor, but she managed to set up a small shop on the island. At age 11, Alexander went to work as a clerk for two New York merchants who had recently settled on St. Croix. When his mother died in 1768, he was cared for by relatives on the island, and continued to work at his clerk job. He was very bright and industrious, and soon worked his way up the ladder from bookkeeper to manager. Friends of the family were so impressed with his ability they sent him to the North American mainland for schooling.

Hamilton enjoyed school, and did very well. He was serious in his studies, and was very, very ambitious. But his studies were interrupted by the coming revolt against England. He quickly threw his support behind the colonies. At age 17 he wrote three well-regarded pamphlets that criticized England for its harsh policies against the American Colonies.

In 1776, as war with Great Britain was breaking out, Hamilton found himself leading soldiers against the English. He showed great bravery. During one battle, he prevented a large army of Redcoats from crossing the Raritan River and attacking George Washington's main army. Washington was very impressed with this young man's abilities.

In February of 1777, Washington asked Hamilton to be his aide-de-camp (a trusted assistant) with the rank of lieutenant colonel. Hamilton was on Washington's staff for four years. The two men became close friends. Washington sent Hamilton on many important missions, and also used him in talks with France, since Hamilton spoke the French language very well. In this way Hamilton gained valuable political and diplomatic experience. During the winters, when most fighting stopped, Hamilton continued his school studies, especially economics and public finance.

In November 1781, with the war nearly over, Hamilton went to Albany, New York, to study law. He quickly became a lawyer in 1782, and the next year started work in New York City. During these years Hamilton also wrote several newspaper articles, urging the new nation to set up a strong central government. In 1786, he was elected to the New York state legislature.

As a member of the New York legislature, Hamilton was sent as a representative to the Continental Congress. (The Continental Congress was where the states made laws before there was a United States, or even a Washington, D.C. These would all come later, after the Constitution was ratified [approved] in 1788.) Hamilton called for another meeting in which representatives from all the states would discuss problems facing the new nation. The meeting he helped bring about was the Constitutional Convention, the true beginning of the United States government as we know it today.

During the Revolutionary War, Hamilton showed great bravery and skill in battle. He became a trusted assistant to General George Washington.

As a delegate to the Constitutional Convention (representing New York), Hamilton did all he could through his writing and meetings with people in power to get a new Constitution created. He was a "Federalist," one who believed in a strong national government. Hamilton's original idea was to have the government be almost like a monarchy, with a president who ruled for life, just like a king. Other delegates decided to soften Hamilton's plan, giving the individual states more rights. Though he didn't get everything he wanted, Hamilton signed his name to the new Constitution.

Some people disliked the new Constitution and started trying to get the states, who had to vote yes or no, to reject it. Hamilton, along with James Madison and John Jay, wrote a series of 85 essays called "The Federalist Papers," defending the Constitution. Hamilton knew that if the states got more power, the Constitution would have little meaning. He said that one of the biggest reasons to have a strong central government was to stop "that secret jealousy which disposes all states to aggrandize [to make greater in power] themselves at the expense of their neighbors." The danger, Hamilton said, was that in fighting for an advantage, the states would harm the United States as a whole.

Hamilton, who wrote about two-thirds of the Federalist Papers, also explained, in clear ways, how the different parts of the new government would work. He talked about the presidency, congress, and the Supreme Court.

The Federalist Papers were very successful. Although written in a hurry, they were widely read and very well respected. In 1788, a ratifying convention was held. Hamilton was a delegate for New York. Due in large part to his hard work, the Constitution was accepted, and the United States as we know it today was born.

When President George Washington took office in April 1789, he needed to quickly fill his cabinet positions, especially the Secretary of the Treasury.

It seemed natural to choose Alexander Hamilton. After all, he was a trusted advisor during the war, was a lawyer with skills in finance and banking, and had a large part in helping create the Constitution. In September, Hamilton started his new job and soon had his hands full making the country financially strong. The decisions he made as Treasury Secretary were made not only because they made good financial sense, but also because they supported Hamilton's political views. Once again, his belief that the federal government should be strong was a major theme.

Hamilton's first step as Secretary was to give the United States good credit. To do this, the federal government assumed (took over) the debt that individual states had accumulated during the war. In this way, the rich men and corporations from which the states had borrowed money would be more closely tied to the federal government. This gave the U.S. Government more power. To handle this money, the new government would need a bank. Hamilton submitted a report, which Washington signed into law, creating the Bank of the United States. Hamilton knew that, through the bank, he could now regulate currency (money), which further increased the federal government's power.

To raise money and to pay off the debt, Hamilton created a system of taxes. This also gave the federal government more power, because the states no longer were the only ones who had the right to tax their citizens. Hamilton also set up a series of taxes, called tariffs, on raw materials and goods the United States imported from other countries. This made foreign merchandise more expensive. Hamilton hoped this would help our own manufacturers, since people would want to buy from them instead of the higher priced imports.

Unlike the Treasury Secretaries of today, Alexander Hamilton had a strong voice in how our new country conducted its foreign policy. Even though we had a Secretary of State (Thomas Jefferson) who was supposed to handle foreign affairs exclusively, Hamilton was a trusted advisor of George Washington. The president listened carefully to what his Treasury Secretary had to say.

Hamilton thought the United States should have better relations with England. He thought trade with England would benefit our economy. Thomas Jefferson, the Secretary of State, thought the United States should be more friendly with France, especially since the French had helped us during our War for Independence. Hamilton, however, hated the French Revolution. (The French Revolution was an overthrow of the French monarchy. It was supposed to give more power to common people.) Hamilton thought this new French government gave too much power to people who were unqualified to lead a nation.

When England and France went to war, Hamilton and Jefferson had a bitter feud over which country the United States should support. President Washington, after listening to both Jefferson and Hamilton, decided that the United States should be neutral, neither supporting nor opposing either side. (This was actually seen as a victory for Hamilton, since the United States had a treaty of alliance with the French at the time. Technically, we should have helped France.)

By 1795, Hamilton had grown tired of his Cabinet position and wished to rebuild his family fortune, which had suffered in the previous years. Hamilton resigned as Treasury Secretary, but was still asked for advice many years afterwards. Five years later, Hamilton–with his political party, the Federalists–tried running for president. But Hamilton had many who disliked him and opposed his policies. They gathered around Thomas Jefferson, and the Federalists were defeated in the election of 1800.

In 1804, Hamilton was challenged to a duel by Aaron Burr, a man who had run for governor of New York and for President of the United States. Hamilton helped defeat him both times. Burr demanded satisfaction for remarks

Hamilton had made about him at a dinner party. His honor at stake, Hamilton accepted the challenge. Early in the morning of July 11, Burr's bullet shot across a dew-laden field and into Hamilton's chest. Hamilton dropped to the ground in pain. "This is a mortal wound, doctor," he said, then fell unconscious. He died the next day.

Hamilton was one of America's first great nationalists. He believed that citizens should give their loyalty to the nation as a whole, not to any one state. Most of his life's work went to making sure the union of the United States was strong. Without his efforts, we would be living in a very different kind of country today.

Hamilton was killed in a famous duel with Aaron Burr in 1804.

Lloyd Bentsen

In late 1992, newly-elected President Bill Clinton had an important choice to make: who to pick for Treasury Secretary? Clinton came into office in large part because he said he wanted to concentrate on America's weak economy. To do the job right, he needed a Treasury Secretary with a lot of experience in finances. Almost as important, though, this person had to be able to work well with Congress in order to push through the President's economic reforms.

Clinton chose Senator Lloyd Bentsen, a Texas Democratic. In choosing Bentsen, Clinton turned to an experienced lawmaker with a cool temper and statesmanlike presence. Bentsen became nationally well known in 1988 when he was the Democratic vice presidential candidate, running along with Michael Dukakis. After the election, many wished that the ticket had been reversed, with Bentsen running for president.

Bentsen has a very deep knowledge of how Congress works. He is a former Senate Finance Committee chairman. He has served in Congress most of his adult life, and had been a Senator for 22 years before taking the Treasury job. He is a master dealmaker. President Clinton hopes that Bentsen can take this experience and cut through the gridlock and red tape that so often stops laws from passing through Congress.

Bentsen has a good memory of financial decisions made by past presidents, both good and bad. He knows how the tax system works, and he has a long record of fiscal responsibility. Some also say that, with his lanky stature and white hair and soothing voice, Lloyd Bentsen even looks like a Treasury Secretary.

Bentsen is more conservative than most Democrats, which means he is more likely to make financial decisions favoring businesses. As the Senate Finance Committee Chairman, he strongly supported tax breaks for real estate companies and oil and gas producers.

Lloyd Bentsen, Treasury Secretary under President Bill Clinton.

Bentsen's experience on the committee also gave him expertise on subjects like Social Security, health policy, and trade. He is well regarded by his colleagues in the Senate and by business people. In Congress, he is liked by both Democrats and Republicans.

In accepting President Clinton's offer to head the Treasury Department, Bentsen said that it wouldn't be easy to leave the Senate. But he said, "I'm comforted by the fact that I'll be representing the President and working for an economic policy that will create jobs in the country". President Clinton knows that in choosing Bentsen, he has a Treasury Secretary that gets things done.

President Clinton introducing Treasury Secretary Lloyd Bentsen.

Glossary

Bullion
Gold or silver in the form of bars, ingots, or plates.

Cabinet
A body of persons appointed by a chief of state or a prime minister to head the executive departments of the government and to act as official advisers.

Congress
The national legislative body of the United States, consisting of the Senate and the House of Representatives. This is the place where laws get made.

Constitution
The system of laws and principles that guide countries on the nature and limits of government. The U.S. Constitution took effect in 1789. It establishes a federal republic with power balanced between the national government and the states. Within the national government, power is separated among three branches: the Executive (President), legislative (Congress), and judicial (Supreme Court). The U.S. Constitution is the supreme law of the land; no other law, state constitution or statute, federal legislation, or executive order can operate in conflict with it.

Counterfeiter
A person who makes fake money, usually with the intent to steal.

Diplomacy
The art or practice of conducting international relations, such as negotiating alliances, treaties, and agreements.

Federalist

A member or supporter of the political party that was formed in the United States in 1787. Federalists favored a strong federal government.

Fiscal Policy

How and how much the government spends money and taxes its citizens.

Foreign Policy

How a country deals with other countries. Deciding to treat Country A as a friend and Country B as an enemy is a foreign policy.

Monarchy

A government ruled by a monarch (for instance, a king or queen).

President-Elect

Presidents are elected in November of an election year, but don't actually take office until Inauguration Day, in January of the following year. Until then, their title is President-elect. They don't have official power yet, but the Secret Service provides them protection.

Tariff

A system of duties (taxes or fees) that a government sets on imported or exported goods. Tariffs are usually used to protect industries in the home country from cheap imports, which harm the business of those industries.

Treaty

An agreement between two or more countries.

Connect With Books

Acheson, Patrician C. *Our Federal Government: How It Works*. New York: Dodd, Mead & Company, 1984.

Cunliffe, Marcus. *The American Heritage History of the Presidency*. American Heritage Publishing Company, 1968.

DeGregorio, William A. *The Complete Book of U.S. Presidents*. New York: Dembner Books, 1984.

Gilfond, Henry. *The Executive Branch of the United States Government*. New York: Franklin Watts, 1981.

Howe, John R. *From Revolution Through the Age of Jackson*. Englewood Cliffs, New Jersey: Prentice-Hall, Inc., 1973.

Parker, Nancy Winslow. *The President's Cabinet and How It Grew*. HarperCollins Publishers, 1991.

Sullivan, George. *How the White House Really Works*. New York: Scholastic, 1990.

The United States Government Manual 1991/1992. Washington, D.C.: Office of the Federal Register, 1991.

Watson, Richard. *Promise & Performance of American Democracy*. New York: John Wiley & Sons, Inc., 1978.

Index